Slices of Life: Couch Potato Pie

Jean Davis

Ramona,
you rock!
Jean

For Barbara

With special thanks to Vergil Davis,

a total babe

(XOXOX)

ACKNOWLEDGMENTS

The following stories were previously published and are reprinted with permission:

How to Clean House Fast, *Sense and non-Sense Weekly Email Newsletter*, February 16, 2013.

Words That Endure, *Sense and non-Sense Weekly Email Newsletter,* July 14, 2013.

Go Fly a Kite! *Voices of American Mothers: Mom to Mom, Sharing Insights, Wisdom and Experience*, Compiled by Beverly Price Nelson, 2013, p. 85.

The Next Generation of Writers and the People Who Love Them, *Odd Duck Society*, October, 2010.

Slices of Life:
Couch Potato Pie

Old family recipe:

Throw whatever life gives you into one big
pot.
Stir things up to mix well.
Press into glass pan.
Bake at moderate temperature.
Keep an eye on what's cooking. From time to
time you might have to adjust the heat.
Be patient. Some things worthwhile could
take forty or fifty years.

When done, keep covered on the back burner.
Serve as needed.

Always plenty
Something sweet for everyone

CONTENTS

Annie, Get My Gun!

Two things I've never wanted in the house were a dog and a gun. I've had bad experiences with both. When I was three, the neighbor's dog chased me into a rose bush. I still have a scar on my shin from it. When I was seven, I watched one of the same neighbor's boxers kill a new pup. He shook it like a rag doll until the puppy was dead. Almost sixty years later I still tend to shy away from dogs that jump, run, lick, bark or wag. I've never considered myself a dog person. Other people can have dogs, but I don't trust canines. And about the gun—I don't even want to get into that. Let's just say our son didn't do it.

So that's a picture of the woman my husband has been married to for forty years. Now look at this snapshot: handsome man, well-kept, wonderful sense of humor, very intelligent. When my husband turned sixty-two, his interests expanded. He started talking about wanting to buy a motorcycle, a handgun, and a dog, all over my strong objections.

The gun and the dog were for our home protection. I could have given him an emphatic "No!" but he looked at me with those gorgeous green eyes of his and said most sincerely, "But I want to do this for you. There have been some break-ins in our area lately, and I don't want to worry about your safety when I travel."

I did not want to embrace his version of home protection, but over the years, I've learned to trust my husband's judgment—like the night our beloved Kitty Baby begged to go outside.

"Don't let her out tonight," my husband said as he left for a meeting. But she cried. I hated to hear her cry. She was so pathetic, and his request was so off-the-wall and unexpected. So I opened the door to appease her and let her out. My husband found her the next day on the side of the road in a pile of slush. She'd been hit by a car. I felt terrible.

I already knew what I'd do in case I ever found myself in a threatening situation. A friend told me a story many years ago about a man with a gun approaching a woman hanging clothes in her back yard. He told her not to say anything but to go back into the house with him. She suspected he planned to rape her.

As they approached the bed, she got down on her knees and invited him to pray with her. Without waiting for his response, she started praying out loud. By the time she finished her prayer, he'd left.

My plan was simple. I would rely on divine intervention. I remembered the Scripture, "Everyone who calls on the name of the Lord will be saved." My plan if anyone broke into the house was to shout "JESUS!" at the top of my lungs. In spite of my husband's concerns, I didn't think I needed a bark alarm, a gun, or ammo.

I listened to my husband's reasoning. I thought I could just humor him and he'd forget about it eventually. He'd been thinking about getting a Yorkie, he said. That surprised both of us. He'd always liked bigger dogs. He kept bringing the idea back up. He wanted me to have a dog, he said, to alert me if someone was on the property. Even a small dog could be helpful.

His persistence and his concern for *me* finally wore me down. A Yorkie wasn't very big. Maybe I could handle a small dog. Maybe it wouldn't lick or bark too much.

The more I thought about it, a Yorkie might be good. I could take a small dog into nursing homes to visit residents. I could begin a nursing home ministry.

So I reluctantly agreed to look at ads for dogs. Little Yorkie and I could be a ministry team, a bright spot for nursing home residents.

Yorkies, we discovered, are expensive. *Very* expensive. We looked at photos of dogs needing homes on local shelter web sites. Maybe not a Yorkie, but a Yorkie-type would be good. I always thought I'd like a dog like Homer, a small mixed-breed our granddaughter's babysitter owned. I liked the way his wiry grey hair stood out at different angles. I liked the way he kept his distance from me. Homer, good dog. Maybe we could find a dog like that, one that pretty much minded its own business.

Finally we located a Homer-almost-look-alike. This dog had unruly hair. We called about the pup and drove ninety miles to a shelter to see it.

The pup, mostly Chihuahua, was named Buster. He came into the room and trotted right past us. He held his head and tail high. He walked tall and proud for such a little guy. But he wouldn't come when I called. He was totally independent, not a people dog. He peed on the carpet, and he was barky. I couldn't imagine myself trying to make friends with a dog that ignored me.

"What about that dog?" I asked the shelter volunteer. He was the most beautiful dog I'd ever seen—white with one brown spot on his back. He let me pet him. He was friendly. I could imagine burying my face in this animal's soft fur. If I had to have a dog, I liked this one.

"Oh, that's Jack. He's been adopted. The new owners are coming in later this afternoon. If you're interested in a pit bull—(Pit bull? Jack was a pit bull?)—then there's a lab/pit mix at the Humane Society they wanted me to take to foster, but I didn't have room. If you want, I can call for an appointment." We did not want a pit bull, but the Humane Society was on our way home. It wouldn't hurt just to stop by and look at their dogs. Maybe they'd have a Yorkie cross.

Well, we did it. The lab/pit was an ordinary looking pup in an extraordinary shelter. She was thirteen weeks old, black with white markings on her chest and feet. Someone had named her Opal, and all the workers knew her. The manager Connie said Opal was her favorite pup. She let us take Opal out to a penned area to walk her. Opal stayed right at our heels. She had such a sweet personality. We went home, slept on it, then called Connie to tell her we'd take her.

"Is this the same dog?" I asked my husband when we returned the next week to pick up our adoptee. "I don't remember her being this big."

"Oh, she won't be very big," he said. "Look how small her feet are."

Opal sat in my lap in the car. I rubbed her soft fur and took in the smell of puppy breath. We stopped for a sandwich on the way home and let Opal out for opportunity to do her business. Another couple approached us. After oohing and ahhing a bit over our new family addition, the woman said, "Oh, look how big her feet are. She's going to be such a big dog." I wondered if it were too late to take our pup back for a refund.

Annie, short for Annie Opal, is now a year old and weighs sixty-five pounds. My husband is the dog owner and in his absence I am the dog sitter. He and Annie developed a wonderful relationship while I kept my distance. He took her for daily walks, got on the floor to play with her. She had too much energy for me. I felt tied down, like I was on a short leash. Someone had to be here every few hours to let the dog out. No more leisurely outings shopping. No more spending the night at our daughter's when my husband was out of town.

As a pup, Annie had very few accidents. She didn't eat *all* my spider plants. She made a hundred-piece puzzle from only two flip-flops, and merely mangled two pairs of prescription eye glasses.

The first few months with the new pup in the house were stressful for me. I went to the emergency room with chest pains. I confess—I worried too much, worried about her jumping on neighbors and knocking down strangers or scratching them. She would not let us touch her feet to trim her toe nails. I was fearful about Annie being full of raw power and exuberance on eye-level with our youngest grandbaby. Were we crazy getting a dog in our senior years?

To add to the stress, our ideas about dog-rearing differed. My husband was more lenient, gave Annie bits of apple, carrot, ice cubes. He let her lick out of the frying pan when he thought I wasn't looking. When he'd sit on the floor with her, she'd lick his fingers, face, ears, neck, the top of his head. What looked like roughhousing bothered me. She responded to my correction of "eeeh," and, in the beginning, I seemed to say that a lot.

After having her for several months now, I've learned to keep myself calm when other people are around her by walking away if I get the overwhelming need to protect the universe from our dog. No one else seems upset with her overtures of friendliness. I just upset myself. "Oh, she's just a pup," they graciously say. Well, of course they'd say that. *They* are dog people. So Annie is not the problem.

Having a pet is supposed to be good for lowering blood pressure. I never needed blood pressure medication until after we got Annie. But maybe that was just coincidence. And when I went to the emergency room with chest pressure, I think it could have been one "eeeh" too many—either that or GERD.

We've had Annie now for ten months. We laugh at her a lot, like this morning, when she had some foreign object perched on the bridge of her nose. Like the way she can carry two toys at one time in her mouth. Or how she can lie on her back and hold a toy between her front feet to play with it.

Annie is predictable and easy to please, and she's smart. If my husband leaves two Frisbees in the yard, she'll remember where they are and get the one she wants to play with. She excels at catching the Frisbee. We can take her out into our unfenced yard and she stays right with us. She loves to ride in the car and makes a good companion for quick trips to the grocery store.

When I'm working at the computer, Annie has a way of staring at the back of my head till I turn around. She can get my attention. And she knows how to put her nose under my wrist if I'm at the computer too long and flick it skyward. She knows where all my buttons are but more and more does a doggie dance on them less frequently.

Annie and I share the love of peanut butter and back rubs. Okay—so maybe I like Annie a little bit. *Finally*. Or a lot. And her bark is probably scary enough to frighten off any intruder. It sure scares me.

She respects my hands-off style of dog rearing, and my heart melts when she approaches me just to rest her head on my leg when I'm watching television. She'll bring me a toy to play fetch, and when she looks up at me with those sweet, brown eyes, I'm a goner. My husband loves her. I love my husband. Annie is the dog he always wanted, he said. He's tolerated so many of my choices in life. How could I deny him the fulfillment of that small life's dream, even if it means sometimes the house smells like dog?

After we got Annie, my husband started looking at guns to complete the second phase of his home protection plan. He pulled up videos on the internet so I could see women shooting guns, women being knocked onto their posterior shooting rifles. Oh, yeah. I really wanted that. I love pain and humiliation. Then he took me to gun shops to let me feel different grips of hand guns. My hands shook. I hyperventilated.

He bought a revolver and I worried about the safety of grandchildren when they came to visit. And what about intruders who use the owner's own gun against them? We went into the back acre of our rural lot to practice shooting. The hand gun wasn't so bad, especially after I discovered I could hit the target. In fact, I found that I liked target practice.

"Can we do this every week-end?" I asked, taking aim at the paper target and slowly squeezing the trigger. Bull's-eye! I think my enthusiasm for shooting may have unnerved my husband.

If I had stayed my ground, he probably wouldn't have made the purchases. But I trust my husband's wisdom. We now have a complete home security system. I have a dog that can bark to alert me. I have a hand gun that I can hold and point, and if my vocal cords don't freeze up, I can shout at any intruder, "I HAVE A GUN AND I KNOW HOW TO USE IT!" right after I yell "JESUS!"

About the motorcycle. Don't get me started on that or about the cigars he started smoking on his sixty-third birthday. Every night, regardless of weather conditions, he sits out on the deck with the dog, curls of smoke rising around his head. He says he's thinking about getting another puppy as a companion for Annie. I might not mind a *small* dog to sit in my lap, but he's thinking Rottweiler. All that smoke curling around his head is clouding his thinking. Mine, too, probably. At first I thought about getting an apartment close by, but now, near retirement, maybe a large house on the backside of a mountain in the Ozarks, with acreage. This house isn't big enough for *four* of us.

Live and Let Live.

How to Clean House FAST!

Do you ever find yourself unmotivated to pick up through the middle of your mess? Here's a proven way you can clean house in thirty minutes or less.

First, choose your friends carefully. You need at least one friend who lives relatively close by who likes to do things on the spur of the moment. Then, when she texts you to say something like "HAPPY VALENTINE'S DAY! Luv U, XOXOX," since you haven't seen her in several weeks, you can text back and ask, "Want to meet for lunch today?" When she says yes, how about 11:30 after her dentist appointment, stay on the computer like you do every day until you have just enough time to shower and get out the door. Then, when you get in your car and discover the engine won't turn over, go back inside the house and text again, saying, "My car battery is dead. Try again next week?" Don't even wait for an answer. Since her dentist's office is only thirty minutes from your house, and though you half hope she won't offer to come get you but know in your heart she probably will, start picking up like crazy.

Take the twelve rolls of toilet paper you bought on sale for your daughter that you've left sitting by the back door out to the car. If only your daughter had time to come visit you or the other way around, she'd have the toilet paper by now. Take the other items you've left by the door—the two bags of books you were going to give to a friend, the WalMart return from Christmas, the sack of used eyeglasses you need to find a depository for, the four bags of give-aways for Good Will, the DVDs you have for your granddaughter—and put them all in the big green plastic container you were using to store items you intended to ask your daughter if she wanted. One big overflowing twenty-gallon tub is less of an eyesore than so many bags of scattered intended "generosity."

Move your husband's cap and gloves from the table and his coat from the back of the chair and drape them artistically over his bicycle in the corner of the room. Take the three stacks of papers, semi-carefully sorted on your dining table, and move them to the folding table you have set up in your home office. Keep them separate from the other three piles already there that you're really really going to sort through as soon as you find time. Take the orange two-gallon bucket filled with water siphoned off from the fish tank the previous weekend from its station by the door and move it outside. Take the blue two-gallon bucket half-filled with turnips from the garden in varying degrees of "aging" and move it out to the wash house. Kick the container of dog food closer to the wall.

In the living room, take the stacks of miscellaneous papers and file folders that have been sitting there since you got bogged down cleaning out your file cabinet two weeks ago and move them to the office, hiding them behind the sofa. Straighten the sofa cushions. While you're in the office, pick up the can of furniture spray you left on top of the credenza the last time you got in a cleaning mood, walk into the living room and get that dust off the top of the entertainment center, then put the furniture spray away.

Comb your hair. When you see your friend pull up, meet her at the car. No need having her walk all the way to the house on such a cold day. Enjoy your lunch. Thank your friend profusely when she brings you home. With your house picked up, you'll be genuinely disappointed she doesn't have time to come in and extend the visit over a cup of tea.

To keep your living quarters in better order, invite your friend over every few weeks for a visit. Mark it on the calendar. Don't wait till thirty minutes before she arrives to start your pick-up in case she makes it a little early. Because that's the kind of friend she is, maybe she'll be willing to help you get those stacks sorted and ride along with you to get the give-aways delivered to their intended destination. All you have to do is ask. That's what friends are for.

Party of Twelve

By the time you read this, our company will have come and gone. Three months ago my husband's sister Sara wrote to say they'd be on their way to visit her husband's sister in New York on June 8. Would my husband be on a business trip? Would we be home?

Of course. I wrote her back and said, "Sure. Come on."

When Sara sent me another e-mail the next day and said, "Oh, by the way. . . ," I began to panic. Oh, by the way, her four boys would be traveling to New York, too—or more correctly, her four boys, their three wives, one fiancé, and the two grandkids. I did a little calculation. The old noggin still computes. That's when I began to worry.

We live in an old house we love, but the floors are sagging and part of the roof on the front porch needs replacing. The kitchen drain is slow and the downstairs toilet won't flush. We live here, but when company comes, especially those who have never been here—the nephews' wives and fiancé in this case, specifically—I like to spruce things up a bit. You know, like pick up the extra two or three pairs of shoes someone left at the front door. Like clean out the refrigerator; power wash the front porch and back deck; wash the shower curtain liner, windows and blinds; paint the living room; shampoo the carpets;   refinish the kitchen cabinets—things like that. Then when company arrives we can let them pretend to believe we always live like this. We know and they probably suspect it isn't so.

It's a little like when you first start gaining weight but can still pull in your tummy. After awhile, when sucking it up no longer works and you give up and start buying elastic waistbands, you just let it all hang out. That's where I am with my body but not yet quite there with my house.

Just to be fair, I do own one pair of jeans with a waistband. The elastic is sewn into the sides.

I had all these "to do's" I wanted my husband to get to—go to the dump, replace a light fixture, take a few pieces of furniture to the storage unit. Nag nag nag. What a joy for him and a headache for me—or the other way around. Twelve weeks till Sara comes. Ten weeks till Sara comes. Four weeks till Sara comes. Somewhere during the week that we were to have company, six days before to be exact, it finally dawned on him. Oh, Sara is coming. Had I made the man deaf?

The person he called to pump out the septic came within hours. Company deserves to be able to flush. He arranged for his friend to come by with his truck and take a load to the dump. That happens tomorrow. Today he made our bathroom beautiful by replacing the ancient fixture. If he doesn't make it to the storage unit, I can always push the sewing machine cabinet back next to the wall by the TV rather than where I've pulled it to in the middle of the walkway so he'd remember.

His waiting to the last minute is definitely a sign of how exercise has kept him youthful. I used to be like that. I used to run right up to the last minute, but now I like to plan things ahead like our ninety-three-year-old friend who likes to get to the barbershop thirty minutes before it opens at 7:00 so he can be first in line. At one time I was amused, but now I understand. I've lived long enough to know sometimes you'd better plan ahead because you just don't know what might happen. What if the school nurse can't reach the grandbaby's mother and she needs me to pick her up from school? What if the grocery store has a run on kale and I have to go to two or three stores before supper to find it?

When Sara comes, where will we put everyone? We have an extra double bed, two singles and two sofas. We have lots of floor space, but who will want to sleep on the floor? And what will I cook for them now that we're vegans? Will everyone like our favorite black bean recipe, or will I need to buy sandwich material for the kids?

A few nights ago my husband called his sister to check on their plans. Maybe we needed to try to rent a few motel rooms. "Rus and I will be there about four on Friday," she said.

"What about the kids?" he asked.

"The kids?" Sara laughed and laughed when my husband told her we thought they were coming, too. Heavens, no. Two of her boys with their wives will be flying to New York and the other two will be driving there directly. She had rented a five-bedroom house on a lake for the week for a family get-together with her boys. She hadn't told us that. She thought it was funny we had misunderstood. A quick re-read of her e-mail left no other interpretation other than we should expect twelve guests.

When my husband hung up, I said, "They're not coming?" I was a little miffed. Wounded, actually. I mean, after all that nagging and no one gets to see the fruit of *that* hard work. Well, Sara and Rus do, but they've been here before. They don't count.

The cabin rental was for a week, Sara said. If we wanted to we could drive up to the lake where they'd be staying and have a chance to visit with everyone. It was only a seven-hour drive.

Only a seven-hour drive? The five-bedroom house she rented sleeps ten or twelve. I relied on my math skills again. Twelve people plus two extra, seven hours in the car times two, and somebody still gets to sleep on the floor.

No, but thanks for inviting us! Maybe next time. I think we're going to stay home and enjoy our clean house.

When in doubt, ask.

Habla – *What?*

Recently I read an article stating people who are fluent in four languages have a lower chance of developing dementia than those who are simply bilingual. If this report is correct, I am doomed. I don't know four languages, nor am I bilingual. According to some people I've met who have trouble understanding my accent, I don't even speak my native language well.

So I did what any other person armed with this new information would do. I got on the internet to find a copy of Rosetta Stone, Spanish. When I saw I couldn't easily afford the investment, even off eBay, I visited the library to see what I could find. Our local library has several sets of foreign language CD's to choose from. I brought home one set of introductory Spanish instruction.

I also checked out a set of CDs for Cantonese. My husband said he might be making a trip to China this year and wouldn't it be nice if he could learn a little Mandarin before the trip. The library didn't have Mandarin CD's, but they did have Cantonese. Mandarin, Cantonese. Surely it doesn't matter. It's all Chinese, right? Hopefully Cantonese will work for him.

I put the first of ten CDs from the basic Spanish set into the CD player. After several minutes of instruction about how to use the course most effectively, the instructor set up the scene by saying a man who speaks English sits by a woman who speaks Spanish. The man wants to strike up a conversation with her. *Oh, I see where this is going*, I think. But I am wrong. First they have to wrestle through who has the dominant understanding of the other's language. Back and forth, back and forth in Spanish they ask and respond.

Do you speak Spanish? No I don't speak Spanish. Do you speak English? No, I don't speak English. For variety, they switch it up. *Do you understand Spanish?* No, he doesn't understand

Spanish, and he doesn't speak Spanish, either. I already know the answer to that one.

As they continue to probe, our dog Annie goes to the back door and barks furiously. I can hardly hear the man's answer to the woman's question, so I turn the volume up. I clearly understand Annie. She is upset.

"Who is this strange man in our house speaking words I don't understand? Where is he?" she barks at me. "Where is he hiding? And why is he talking so loud? And why are you talking back to a man I can't see?" Though I still may not be able to speak her language after four years of living with Annie, I clearly understand the language of lab/pit bull. And I'm convinced she understands my every English word, Southern accent and all. She is such a smart girl.

My job as a foreign language student is to repeat every phrase the man and woman say, but it's difficult to concentrate because I am worried about this couple. He wants to ask her a question but he can't get past the language barrier. Maybe he is enthralled with her beauty. Maybe he wants to ask her for a date. Ah, the language of love!

Perhaps that's not it at all. Maybe he's lost in a strange city. Maybe he has a headache and needs directions to a pharmacy. After several minutes of their dialogue, I have a headache. I am frustrated by their inability to communicate. I want to yell, "Just say it already! Use sign language, for Pete's sake!"

I am glad my husband is at work and no one is at home but the dog. I feel a little self-conscious trying these new phrases out loud. Ten minutes into the CD I am instructed to mimic the Spanish-speaking woman's attempt of "Sir, do you understand Spanish?" I give it the old college try.

Annie is quiet now and sitting in the room with me. I look into her dark brown eyes.

"Perdón, Señor. ¿Entiende español?" I ask. She tilts her head first one way, then the other. She seems confused.

"No entiende español," I repeat after the man. Evidently Annie doesn't understand Spanish, either. She gets up from where she's sitting and moves closer to me. She's never heard this directive before. She is a female English-understanding dog, and I'm addressing her in a language foreign to her velvety floppy ears. She is so attentive I can tell she wants to understand. She really does.

"Perdón, Señor," I repeat. "¿Entiende español?" Annie lies down at my feet and slowly rolls over, exposing her belly. I have intimidated her. I start to laugh. Oh, to get others to lie down and roll over so easily!

Unable to carry on this dialog while laughing so hard, I stop the CD. First, I have to catch my breath. Poor Annie. Perhaps she will understand better if I address her more correctly. I try again.

"Perdón, *Señorita*. ¿Entiende español?" She answers by leaving the room. Perhaps I have hurt her feelings. She probably knows I am laughing at her, not with her, since she's not laughing at all. I'm just part way through the first lesson. Already our dog is throwing in the towel. Maybe I should take the hint and follow suit.

I shut my eyes so I can concentrate on the lesson. I rest my chin on my hands. When I wake up, I'm already twenty-six minutes into the thirty-minute CD. One thirty-minute session down and nine more to go with this introductory set of CD's, then I'll be ready to start the killer course in Spanish once this set is returned to the library.

I'm almost ready to move on to Cantonese. If the CD cover is accurate, I should be speaking Cantonese in six easy lessons. If I had realized

Spanish would be this hard, I would have started with Cantonese first. Then I can check out other foreign language sets available at our library. If speaking four languages might deter dementia, imagine the benefits of knowing five or six—if I don't develop an ulcer first. I wonder how far I need to advance past "Excuse me, sir. Do you speak English, Spanish, Cantonese, Italian, French, or German?" to have any benefit against dementia?

"¿Habla español?" the English-speaking man on the CD asks again as the first lesson comes to a close.

"No!" I answer emphatically in my best Spanish accent. Then I turn off the CD and head upstairs to take a nap. But first, I need to stop by the kitchen for ibuprofen.

Words That Endure

In the many years my husband and I were active in church, we heard hundreds of sermons but only remember two well.

The first was delivered in a community church in rural Arkansas, 1974. The pastor said he didn't have much time to prepare his sermon that morning because his cows got out, so the topic of the day was Birds of the Bible. *Birds of the Bible.* Though I don't remember the birds except for a couple of sparrows and one raven, I've remembered the topic all these years. When it comes to mind, I always smile. Who would have known cows breaking out of a preacher's fence one Sunday morning in Arkansas would still create joy in Delaware almost four decades later? It's like a family joke. My husband or I can say "birds of the Bible" in the other's presence, and we'll both chuckle.

The next unforgettable sermon was delivered in a large old-line denominational church in Starkville, Mississippi, ten years later. The assistant pastor didn't preach often, but my husband and I can quote from memory twelve words he shared. Three things a man or woman needs, he said: Something to do, someone to love, and something to look forward to. He didn't give chapter and verse for that, and if I remember correctly, he attributed the phrase to that great man of God, Merv Griffin. A little research on Google also attributes the quote to Elvis Presley, Rita Mae Brown, Maya Angelou, and Immanuel Kant who, by the way, died in 1804. From his death date, I'm guessing Kant may be closer to the original source.

You never know. If something happens in life that causes you distress, like, let's say the cows get out, maybe your circumstance will have a ripple effect and in some way minister to others. It could happen. And let's say you're all in a panic because you didn't have time to prepare what you'd intended so you pull something together and hope for the best. It's all purposeful.

Sometimes when my husband or I have felt stuck, one of us has acknowledged we'll be okay. We have something to do, someone to love, and something to look forward to. Those are three things we can remember and hold on to. And if circumstances really get unsettling, we can always go out and check on the birds of the Bible.

"Look at the birds of the air; they do not sow or reap or store away in barns, and yet your heavenly Father feeds them. Are you not much more valuable than they?" (Matthew 6:26).

Today in my little anxious heap I am remembering fences that need mending, errant Herefords, and common sparrows. I am grateful for words that have endured.

Keep it simple.

Why More Men Don't Teach Elementary School

My husband Vergil came in from a thirty-mile bike ride and waited for me to get ready to go with him to buy bedding plants. "We won't be gone long," Vergil said.

The proprietor, Alicia, was on the phone when we got there, so we waited. She'd just gotten news that her mother might have had a stroke. We talked parental health, what she should do. We talked tomato plants, then bedding plants, then bee hives. (It's a long story.)

As soon as we got in the car to go home, Vergil said, "I'm in so much pain!" It seems that on top of the two cups of coffee Vergil drank while waiting for me to get ready, he had also consumed two bottles of water on his bike ride.

"Do what other people do. Just pull over and go behind some bushes," I said, trying to be helpful.

"I can't hide behind those bushes! I'll just hurry. It's just six more miles."

After a few more comments, he said, "I'm in so much pain I can't talk." Then he said what he really needed to tell me. "I'm in so much pain I can't listen."

I placed a hand on my husband's shoulder. On the back road home we pulled up behind a maroon van doing about thirty miles an hour. Then Vergil did something totally out of character for him. It was obvious to me he was out of his mind with the building pressure.

"You #%&*!! Get off the road if you can't drive any faster than that!" Then Vergil whipped the car around him.

I was doubled up in laughter when I remembered that a man who is feeling so much abdominal pressure that he can't talk or listen certainly doesn't need to be trying to suppress laughter. I got hold of myself. When we pulled into our driveway, Vergil quickly exited.

And that's why more men don't teach elementary school. Their bladders are too small.

Everyone who has ever taught young children knows you'd better go before you leave home because chances are you'll never get another opportunity until the last child leaves campus. Though men may have a desire to teach early grades, though they may have hearts as big as Montana and heads full of knowledge and expertise in the latest classroom management techniques, men have smaller bladders than women. Can you imagine the mounting pressure in the elementary classroom? Two cups of coffee before work and a bottle or two of water, then for no apparent reason, the teacher can't talk, can't listen, and can't tolerate someone moving at a slow speed.

Of course, regular breaks could be integrated into a teacher's schedule. As far as I know, that's not practiced, but it probably should be on behalf of those kids who need at least one grown-up male role model in their lives.

Always go before you leave home.

Hiring Jenny
(2008)

When I go to my daughter's house to baby-sit, Jenny is there. She is amazing. She washes and folds clothes and puts them away, picks up after the kids, loads the dishwasher, provides transportation, helps with homework. If I'm there six or eight hours, Jenny works the whole time and never sits down unless it's behind the wheel when she picks up the oldest child from school or when she makes a quick trip to the grocery store to buy what she notices my daughter is out of.

Jenny has such energy. When I come home from babysitting, I'm worn out. I can let dishes sit overnight. I don't have that many clothes to wash since it's just the two of us, my husband and me.

And I can easily let stacks of stuff sit for months. Okay, *years* in closets and attic. We've lived in this house fourteen years, and it's possible I still haven't unpacked some of the moving boxes.

Obviously Jenny cares deeply for my daughter, a single mom, and her three kids. I'm sure love is the motivator. I need someone to love me like Jenny loves Libby. So the last time I was at my daughter's, I decided to invite Jenny over to help me out, too.

This morning, Jenny showed up just as my feet hit the floor. What a whiz that woman is! She's already straightened the kitchen and the desk by the computer. She trimmed dead leaves off house plants and watered the plants in the flower beds. She swept the front porch. I've needed someone who has fresh eyes to see my old mess, someone to love me as much as I love my daughter and grandchildren. I mean, as much as *Jenny* loves my daughter and grandchildren.

I try to practice the golden rule, treating others the way I want them to treat me. Maybe it's time to treat myself with the same love and compassion I have for others.

Oh. By the way, today just call me Jenny. I hope I can keep her around every day.

Go Fly A Kite!

When our son Sam was five, we lived down a dirt road in a rented farmhouse on twenty acres in rural Missouri. Our landlord, my husband's business partner, had cross fences, a horse, cattle, and a pond for fishing on the property. We had a large garden and also kept rabbits and chickens.

One day Sam came to me and said, "Mama, come outside. Help me fly a kite." You know the mother answer, right?

"Sorry, Sam. I'm busy." I *was* busy. I looked at the clock over the kitchen sink. My husband would be home in about an hour. Before he got in, I wanted to pick up again through the middle of the house, fold another load of laundry, and finish supper. I recited my list to this boy of ours.

I've played this scene over and over again in my mind. I still remember how he looked up at me with those big brown eyes of his and said those words I haven't been able to get out of my head for the thirty years that have followed this incident.

"But Mom," he said. "I want you to do things *with* me, not for me." How could one so young have so much wisdom?

Well, you know what I did, don't you? I set the towels to be folded aside, went out to let the sun warm my face, and helped a small boy make a good memory. I had to overcome my sense of ineptitude and foolishness since I'd never actually flown a kite.

I remember my nervous laughter at our first attempts. I was elated as our efforts showed promise, then my hope would be dashed as the kite took a nose dive and skidded against the ground, time after time. But finally we caught the breeze just right. Sam's face was filled with wonder as the strips of old sheeting tied on as a tail to the 24-inch square of navy-and-red paper magic made figure eights against the background of a clear blue sky. I hope Sam's spirit soared like the kite we finally got up in the air. I know mine did.

If I have any advice for mothers who still have children at home, it would be this: Take time from your schedules to do things *with* your kids, not just for them. Go fly a kite! Some day you'll need that memory.

Do things with those you love,
not just for them.

Being (Almost) Famous

Another Sam story:

Again, when Sam was five, he took me by surprise one day when he said, "Mama, do you know who you look like? You look just like Dolly Parton, except . . ."

Did he already realize what Dolly was famous for? I held my breath, waiting to see how he would finish. ". . . except, Mama, your hair is shorter." Oh, my sweet boy.

That was thirty years ago when Dolly weighed thirty or forty pounds more than she does now and I weighed thirty or forty pounds less than I do currently. Sure, I might be able to see the similarity if I had a better imagination. But at 5'4", I'm taller, and I've always lacked, well, you know, any of Dolly's tremendous, mmm, talent.

I wonder if someone in Dolly Parton's life has ever said to her, "You know, you remind me a lot of Jean Davis, except . . ." Would she hold her breath waiting for someone to fill in the blank? Would she scratch her wig and say, "Who?" Would she double up in laughter?

Oh, to be loved by a child!

What I Have to Deal With

I wasn't able to send an e-mail, so I asked Vergil how I'd know if I needed to poke the hole in the little box that was with the computer.

"What?" he said.

I repeated myself. "I couldn't get an e-mail to go through. Is this when I need to use a paperclip to poke the hole in the little box that's with the computer?"

He repeated *himself.* "What?" he asked again.

After another try or two to get him to understand—and I couldn't understand why he couldn't understand since he'd done the task so many times himself—I motioned for him to follow me into the computer room.

I pointed at the computer. I spoke a little louder. I never noticed Vergil was hard of hearing.

"I can't get an e-mail to go through. The message that pops up on the computer screen says it can't find our server." Then I pointed at the little box with the flashing lights that Vergil sometimes pokes with a paper clip.

"Oh," Vergil said. "Jean, the way you ask the question is, 'Do I need to reset the modem?'" He looked at me for a moment, then said, "Or, you could say, 'Do I need to use a paper clip to poke the little hole on the little box that is by the computer?'"

I'm glad he's coming around to seeing things my way.

Finally.

The Next Generation of Writers and the People Who Love Them

Grandma, we have to write a book. Aidan Davis

One night while visiting my daughter's family, I read one of my favorite Golden Books to my grandchildren. More accurately, I *tried* to read to them. Seven-year-old Aidan kept interrupting me.

"Can you help me look for *Diary of a Wimpy Kid,* book 3? I checked it out from the library."

"I haven't seen it, but I'll look," I promised.

"If I don't find it, I have to pay fourteen dollars."

"That's a lot of money."

"I know. . . . Grandma, maybe we can write a book. We can write the book together, then I can be the illustrator," he said. "That's the one who draws the pictures, right?"

"Right."

"And what's the guy called who writes the story?"

"The author," I said.

"Oh, yeah. I can write a book, and I can draw pictures."

"I want to write a book," his younger sister wailed.

"Okay. We can write two books," Aidan told her, then, "Oh, Grandma, we can write lots of books, and we can sell them on eBay. We can sell the ones on eBay you think are most awesome.

"I have the paper," he said, showing me a full ream of copy paper. I was impressed. "I can start the book tonight and finish it tomorrow." Now I was very impressed. I've been working on a novel off and on for years.

Later I went to Aidan's room to check on his progress.

"How's it going, Bud?" I asked. He sat at his desk and stared out the window.

He sighed. "I can't think of anything to write." I knew the feeling.

I checked my watch—twelve minutes till bedtime. "You need pajamas," I said. "I do my best writing in my pajamas." He dutifully put on red super hero pj's and went back to work.

Bent over a quarter-inch stack of blank paper with pencil in hand, he asked, "How do you spell 'diary'?" I spelled it for him. "How do you spell 'wimpy'?" he asked. When he asked how to spell "kid," I knew we might not *completely* finish writing the book by his projected deadline, tomorrow. After all, it was bedtime.

The next afternoon when he got in from school, Aidan dropped his backpack by the door. "We need to work on our book," he said first thing.

"Did you think of a story to write?" I asked as he searched the pantry for a snack.

"No. Did you?" I shook my head.

"Write a story about what you know," I told him. "You like to play sports and ride bikes. You like to go fishing."

Aidan answered a knock at the door. A boy about my grandson's age came in.

"This is J.J.," Aidan said. "We're going outside to play." So much for story writing. Aidan grabbed his baseball glove and bat. Oh, I see. He was going to do research.

After a two-day visit, I left my daughter's gratified that one of my grandchildren wants to be a writer, too. Besides a passion for writing and illustrating, Aidan already has a marketing plan. His occasional financial need will keep him motivated. He's an avid reader, and he knows how to do research. All he needs now is a little help with spelling—and a story.

I can see it now. I'll have to get someone to help me set up a PayPal account for eBay. Aidan is computer-savvy, so he can probably help me. And I may need to dip into my savings. I predict there will be awesome books to buy in my future.

Moving On

When my writer friend Barbara moved to Florida, I felt sadness, of course, because she is such a good friend and we did so much together. Neither one of us had proved to be very good at using the phone, but we'd see each other every week or two. We wrote together, ate together, and went to the movies and the library. We shared favorite authors. We laughed a lot. Now she is fourteen hours away by car but always in my thoughts and heart.

Memories of time spent with Barbara warms my heart. When we'd get together for lunch, Barbara would choose one of three places. I could suggest another restaurant, but she'd been there once, she said, and the food wasn't really that good. I had to agree. I couldn't go to IHOP after she moved. We'd eaten there so often someone would surely ask, "Where's your friend?" and I knew I'd have trouble choking out the word, "Florida."

Eighteen years my senior—and I am no spring chicken—Barbara shared acquired wisdom. The mother of six children, she once told me when I was crying on her shoulder, "Jean, you have to let your kids make their own mistakes." I knew taking my hands off was the right thing to do, but oh, so difficult.

When I got a little teary telling her good-bye, Barbara said, "You'll live, and so will I." She sees this move as the last one she'll make before the Big One. The week before loading up the U-Haul, I helped her pack one day and clean another. It was an act of selfishness on my part. For a few mores hours, I had a chance to be with Barbara.

So, what did I do with my time those first few weeks spent missing her? I tackled the rooms upstairs sorting keeps, throw-aways, and give-aways. We have a lot of stuff. I wanted to be ready to move, just in case I could convince my husband to move to Florida. Though I was sad for myself, I was happy for her. Her life is very full. She's living close to so many family members.

One thing that binds us to others is shared laughter. Before another friend, Judy, moved to Georgia, we had one glorious evening where she and a mutual friend and I sat in her living room and laughed till tears flowed and we could barely catch our breath. Recalling the memory of that evening always makes me chuckle. I don't even know now what we were laughing about, but I happened to look out her front window to see two of her neighbors walking by looking in the window to see what was going on. And seeing their curiosity, of course, made us laugh all the more.

When I also think of Peggy who moved upstate, I remember walking with her through a difficult time, but what comes to the forefront are the mornings we'd meet for breakfast. I remember her cinnamon pancakes, my eggs, bacon, toast, and coffee, and always, always the laughter.

We are tied to others through shared genes, affinities, struggles, and heartaches, but joy survives. When we make our final move, the Big One, I'm sure though we may leave others saddened by our departure, hopefully even in the midst of missing us, they'll be able to remember happy moments we've shared. May those memories ease their ache and make them smile.

About the Author

Jean Davis has published inspirational stories, poems, and devotions. Her book of Christmas stories, *Happy Birthday, Jesus, and Other Things I Can't Say*, is available on Amazon. She and her husband Vergil live in Delaware with their dog Annie.

jeandaviswrites@yahoo.com